MW01489942

I Am:

Embracing My Identity as His Beloved Daughter

With questions at the end of each chapter for groups or personal study.

Written by Jackie DaHora, LCSW

TherapeaceCounseling.Org

Scripture quotations taken from the (NASB®) New American Standard Bible®, Copyright © 1960, 1971, 1977, 1995, 2020 by The Lockman Foundation. Used by permission. All rights reserved. Lockman.org

Scripture quotations are from the ESV® Bible (The Holy Bible, English Standard Version®), copyright © 2001 by Crossway, a publishing ministry of Good News Publishers. Used by permission. All rights reserved. The ESV text may not be quoted in any publication made available to the public by a Creative Commons license. The ESV may not be translated in whole or in part into any other language.

Disclaimer:

This book is an educational resource, not a substitute for professional counseling or therapy.

ISBN: 9798395838933
Independently published

CONTENTS

DEDICATION

To my mom who sacrificed so much, my sister who continuously shows zeal for spiritual growth, and my dad who is embracing Christ's love more and more each day.

ACKNOWLEDGMENTS

I would like to thank my husband, who leads our home passionately in pursuit of Jesus Christ.

Introduction

Today, us women face many challenges and pressures that can leave us feeling lost, insecure, and inadequate. Societal expectations, personal struggles, and the constant noise of news and social media, can make it difficult for us to find our true selves and understand our worth.

For years, I have counseled women seeking help due to anxiety, depression, stress, and other issues. What I've discovered is that typically there's a lack of knowledge on spiritual identity; they don't know who God says they are and this exacerbates their symptoms and hinders their healing. Hosea 4:6 (ESV) says, "My people are destroyed for lack of knowledge."

We are going to delve into sixteen powerful affirmations that will help you connect with your inner strength, embrace your uniqueness, and discover the person God says you are. Each chapter explores an affirmation beginning with the words "I am...", focusing on different aspects of your identity, personal growth, and relationship with God.

By reflecting on these affirmations and the accompanying Biblical teachings, you will be able to identify the lies you have believed and will gain new insights into your divine purpose. You may realize you have areas or wounds that need healing and surrendering. You will be equipped with practical tips and exercises to help you integrate these affirmations into your daily life.

I also encourage you to utilize the Mental Health Tools and Spiritual Disciplines list (pg.87) to supplement each chapter. There is also a "Steps to Reframing Negative Thoughts with Biblical Principles" (pg.95) Another helpful resource is to speak to someone for support such as a leader, pastor, or counselor from your church. You can also reach out to us and we'd be happy to help you or connect you with someone.

In "I Am" you will be reminded that you are not alone in your struggles, and that God is always with you, guiding and supporting you every step of the way. You will be empowered to face life challenges with confidence. You will be inspired to celebrate your unique gifts and talents, to let go of fear and self-doubt, and to embrace the extraordinary person God created you to be.

Whether you are a woman of faith seeking to deepen your relationship with God or someone who is simply searching for a deeper understanding of your true self, this book offers a transformative and uplifting experience that will help you redefine your identity and discover the powerful woman within.

As you journey through the chapters of "I Am," you will find strength in the knowledge that God's love and wisdom are always with you, shaping your path and guiding your steps. Allow yourself to be embraced by God's grace and let your spirit soar as you uncover the truth about who you are and the incredible purpose you were created for.

Embrace the journey and allow the words of this book to guide you, uplift you, and inspire you as you uncover the divine truths about your identity and your purpose. In the end, you will emerge stronger, more confident, and filled with a renewed sense of self-worth and love.

Grab your pen, highlighter and bible, and let's begin!

Chapter 1 - I am Forgiven

The core of who we are as men of God is built on the forgiveness we receive through Jesus Christ. It's a powerful truth that can be hard to fully grasp: when we confess our sins and put our faith in Him, we are not only forgiven but also made new. Our past mistakes and failures no longer define us. Instead, we are surrounded by God's love and grace, which sets us free.

1 John 1:9 says, "If we confess our sins, He is faithful and just to forgive us our sins and purify us from all unrighteousness." This isn't just a religious statement—it's a personal promise. Forgiveness isn't something we have to earn; it's a free gift given to us through faith in Jesus. As forgiven men, we are called to live with purpose, using our unique gifts to serve God and others.

Let's be real: embracing our identity as forgiven men can be tough. The world often points out our flaws and failures, making us feel unworthy. Our own thoughts can be full of doubt and fear, questioning our worth in God's eyes. The enemy tries to confuse us about who we are in Christ by whispering lies that make us doubt ourselves.

That's why this chapter is so important. It's not just about knowing we are forgiven; it's about living in that forgiveness. It's about letting go of guilt and shame and stepping into the freedom that comes from knowing we are loved and accepted by God.

Whether you've known God for years or are just starting your journey, understanding God's forgiveness is the starting point that shapes our entire lives. Let's explore what it means to be forgiven, how to overcome the challenges to believing this, and how to live as confident, forgiven men who show Jesus' grace and love to others.

Three Influences on Our Understanding of Forgiveness

What the World Says: Society often pushes us to find our value in our achievements, careers, or possessions, leading to constant comparison and feelings of insecurity. But our identity as forgiven men is based on God's unconditional love, not on anything external. When the world tells us we're not enough, we can remember Colossians 1:13-14: "For He has rescued us from the dominion of darkness and brought us into the kingdom of the Son He loves, in whom we have redemption, the forgiveness of sins."

What We Tell Ourselves: Sometimes, we are our own worst critics. We might struggle with guilt or self-doubt, questioning if we're truly forgiven. It's important to realize that these thoughts don't define us. Instead, we must hold onto the truth in Scripture, like Psalm 103:12: "As far as the east is from the west, so far has He removed our transgressions from us." By focusing on God's Word and replacing negative thoughts with His truth, we find freedom and healing.

What the Enemy Says: The devil tries to undermine our confidence in God's love and forgiveness by filling our minds with lies. To fight this, we need to stand firm in our faith and use God's Word. 1 Peter 5:8-9 warns us to "be alert and of sober mind. Your enemy the devil prowls around like a roaring lion looking for someone to devour. Resist him, standing firm in the faith." As we resist these lies and hold onto God's promises, we can walk confidently in our identity as forgiven men.

Practical Steps to Living Out Your Forgiven Identity

Build a Daily Relationship with God: Spend time in prayer, reading the Bible, and worshiping God. Talk to Him throughout your day about your thoughts, feelings, hopes, and fears. Let the truth of His Word transform your heart and mind. If negative thoughts come up, like

"You're not good enough because...," respond with, "Yes, I did that, AND Jesus forgave me."

Live with Purpose: Set goals that align with God's plan for your life, and look for ways to serve others. Not sure where to start? Focus on the greatest commandment: "Love the Lord your God with all your heart, soul, and mind. And love your neighbor as yourself" (Matthew 22:37-39).

Share Your Faith: Be bold in sharing your story and the good news of Jesus' forgiveness with others. If you feel unsure, write out your testimony. Keep it simple—just a couple of minutes long. For example: "When I was young, I went to church but didn't have a real relationship with God. At 17, I learned about His love and realized I needed to confront my sins. I couldn't earn my way to heaven; only Jesus' sacrifice could give me forgiveness. That truth changed my life, and now I live to serve Him."

As we continue this journey, let's never forget the power of God's forgiveness. We are forgiven, redeemed, and made new through Christ. Let's walk confidently in this truth and declare, "I am forgiven."

Chapter 1 - I am Forgiven

Group/Individual Questions

What does forgiveness mean to you personally?

Can you recall a time when you struggled to accept God's forgiveness? What helped you to finally accept it?

How has embracing God's forgiveness changed your life?

What steps can you take to remind yourself of God's forgiveness when you're feeling guilty or ashamed?

How can you extend the same forgiveness you've received to others in your life?

How does God's forgiveness shape your understanding of grace?

Chapter 2 - I am Safe

Safety is a word that resonates deeply with all of us. It's a fundamental human need that shapes our lives from the earliest stages of childhood. As we grow and develop, our understanding of safety evolves, encompassing not only physical protection but also emotional and psychological well-being. Yet, for many, the feeling of safety can be elusive, especially if our past is marked by experiences that have left us feeling vulnerable or threatened.

In an instant we may encounter moments that trigger our inner child, awakening memories of unsafe moments from our past. These triggers can manifest in various ways, such as anxiety, fear, or even physical symptoms. They remind us that the quest for safety is not merely about avoiding physical harm; it's about healing the wounds that may linger beneath the surface, reaching into the very core of who we are.

But where can we find true safety? How can we navigate the complexities of life with a sense of security and peace? The answer, as we will discover in this chapter, lies in our relationship with God, and inviting him in any areas where we may feel unsafe- past, present and future.

From a mental health standpoint, safety is deeply connected to our inner world. Our past experiences, particularly those involving trauma or fear, can shape our perception of safety. Childhood memories of neglect, abuse, or instability may linger into adulthood, manifesting as anxiety, depression, or other mental health challenges. These past traumas can create barriers that hinder our ability to feel safe, even in environments that are objectively secure.

Understanding and addressing these underlying issues is crucial. Therapy, counseling, and self-care practices can be instrumental in healing these wounds, helping us to rebuild a sense of safety from the inside out. By acknowledging and working through our past, we can create a foundation of emotional security that supports our overall well-being.

From a biblical perspective, safety takes on an even deeper take. It's about finding refuge and assurance in something greater than ourselves - in the loving embrace of God. The Bible is rich with promises of God's protection, care, and love.

Verses like Psalm 46:1, "God is our refuge and strength, an ever-present help in trouble," remind us that our ultimate safety is not found in our circumstances, possessions, or human relationships, but in our relationship with the Creator. These words are more than poetic expressions; they are assurances that we can cling to, knowing that our safety is not dependent on our circumstances but on the unchanging character of God.

This safety is not a fleeting emotion or a temporary state; it's a profound truth that we can anchor our lives to. No matter what storms we face, no matter what fears or doubts may assail us, we can find peace and security in knowing that God is with us. His love is unchanging, His power is unshakable, and His promises are unbreakable. In Him, we are not merely protected from physical harm; we are held, cherished, and loved beyond measure. This realization can transform our lives, freeing us from fear and empowering us to live with confidence, purpose, and joy unlike living in this world can often feel chaotic and unpredictable, and it's easy for fear and anxiety to take root in our hearts.

In times of uncertainty, we may find ourselves searching for stability and protection, longing for a safe haven where we can feel secure and at peace. Feeling safe can be difficult to obtain when we receive conflicting messages from the world, our own thoughts, and the devil's lies. Let's examine these three sources and learn how to combat their influence on our understanding of safety:

What the world says: The world often encourages us to find our safety in our finances, our jobs, careers, our relationships, or ourselves. As women of faith, we can find solace in the knowledge that God is our refuge and fortress, providing us with a sense of safety and security that transcends the uncertainties of the world around us.

What we tell ourselves: Our thoughts can cause us to feel alone and unprotected. We may struggle with fear based thoughts that tell us we are alone. By placing our trust in God, we can overcome fear and anxiety and embrace the feeling of safety that comes from knowing we are protected by the Creator of the universe.

What the devil says: The devil seeks to hinder our ability to feel safe in God by reminding us of tragic events in our past, current events in the news, or instilling fear about the future. The Bible offers us a powerful promise of safety in the presence of God. In Psalm 91:1-2, we read: "He who dwells in the secret place of the Most High shall abide under the shadow of the Almighty. I will say of the LORD, 'He is my refuge and my fortress; my God, in Him I will trust.'"

In the story of Ruth, we see a beautiful example of a woman who found safety in the arms of God. Ruth was a Moabite who chose to follow her mother-in-law Naomi back to Israel after the death of her husband. As a foreigner in a strange land, Ruth faced many challenges and uncertainties, but she chose to trust in the God of Israel and cling to the hope that He would provide for her and Naomi. Through her faith and perseverance, Ruth found safety and security in the love and protection of Boaz, a kind and godly man who eventually became her husband. Their story illustrates the power of God's provision and protection for those who place their trust in Him.

In order to cultivate a sense of safety in our lives, we must actively choose to trust in God and rely on His promises. This involves daily practices such as prayer, meditation on Scripture, and affirming God's presence in our lives. By doing so, we can begin to internalize the truth that we are safe in God's hands, regardless of the challenges and uncertainties we may face.

Here are some practical steps you can take to help you feel more secure and safe in your relationship with God:

1. Meditate on Scripture: Spend time each day reading and reflecting on passages from the Bible that speak to God's protection and provision. As you meditate on these truths, allow them to sink into your heart and mind, giving you a sense of safety and assurance. Psalm 91:1-2, Psalm 46:1, Proverbs 18:10, Isaiah 41:10, 2 Samuel 22:3-4, Nahum 1:7, Psalm 4:8

2. Pray for protection: Make it a habit to pray for God's protection and guidance in your life. Ask Him to surround you with His presence and to help you feel secure in His love.

3. Create a safe space: Establish a designated area in your home where you can go to pray, read Scripture, and connect with God. This can be a quiet corner, a small room, or even a closet. Make this space a sacred place where you can retreat to when you need to feel safe and secure.

4. Surround yourself with supportive people: Build relationships with other women of faith who can encourage you, pray with you, and remind you of God's love and protection. Together, you can support one another in your journey toward feeling safe in God's arms.

We can find solace in the knowledge that God is our refuge and fortress, providing us with a sense of safety and security that transcends the uncertainties of the world around us. By placing our trust in Him, we can overcome fear and anxiety and embrace the feeling of safety that comes from knowing we are protected by the Creator of the universe.

Let us hold onto the promises of God and make it a daily practice to trust in Him. By cultivating a sense of safety in our lives through prayer, meditation on Scripture, creating a safe space, and building supportive relationships, we can experience the peace that comes from knowing we are safe in His arms.

So today, let us boldly declare, "I am safe," and walk confidently in the knowledge that we are protected and secure in God's love.

Chapter 2 - I am Safe

Group/Individual Questions

How do you define safety in your life?

Can you share a time when you felt God's protective love in your life?

How does knowing that you are safe in God's love affect your daily life?

What can you do to cultivate a greater sense of safety and security in God's love?

How can you help others to experience the safety found in God's love?

Chapter 3 - I am Healed

Healing is a profound need that resonates with all of us. Whether physical, emotional, or spiritual, the journey towards healing is a complex and deeply personal process. The Bible is rich with stories of healing, demonstrating God's compassion and desire to restore us to wholeness. One such story is that of the woman who touched Jesus' garment, found in Mark 5:25-34. Her persistence, belief, and ultimate healing through Christ's power provide a beautiful illustration of the healing available to all who seek Him.

The woman in the story had been suffering from a bleeding disorder for twelve years. Despite seeking help from many doctors, her condition only worsened. When she heard about Jesus, she believed that if she could just touch His clothes, she would be healed. Her faith and persistence led her to Jesus, and as soon as she touched His garment, her bleeding stopped. Jesus acknowledged her faith, saying, "Daughter, your faith has healed you. Go in peace and be freed from your suffering." Her story emphasizes the importance of persistence, belief, and recognizing who Christ is in our healing journey.

Emotional and spiritual healing is also a vital aspect of our overall well-being. When we invite Jesus into our lives, it's essential to surrender every area, including the closed doors of our past. By allowing Him access to those hidden places, we open ourselves to profound healing and transformation. Jesus doesn't merely want to be a part of our lives; He wants to permeate every aspect, bringing healing, peace, and restoration to even the deepest wounds. This surrender is a continuous process, a daily decision to trust Him with all that we are.

What the world says: Society often promotes quick fixes, self-help techniques, and a focus on external sources of happiness as the keys to healing. However, true healing comes from the transformative power of God's love and grace. When the world offers superficial solutions, we can turn to God's Word for the truth of His healing power.

What we tell ourselves: Our thoughts can be a significant barrier to healing. We may struggle with feelings of unworthiness, guilt, or shame, making it difficult to accept God's healing. To overcome these thoughts, we must remind ourselves of the truth found in Scripture, such as Psalm 147:3, which says, "He heals the brokenhearted and binds up their wounds."

What the devil says: The devil seeks to hinder our healing by planting doubts and lies in our minds. He may whisper that our pain is too great or that we are undeserving of healing. To combat these lies, we must stand firm in our faith, armed with the Word of God, and remember the promise in James 4:7: "Submit yourselves, then, to God. Resist the devil, and he will flee from you."

Practical Steps to being healed:

1. Acknowledge your need for healing: Be honest with yourself and with God about the areas in your life where you need healing.
2. Meditate on Scripture: Spend time each day reading and reflecting on passages from the Bible that speak to God's healing power. Isaiah 53:5, Psalm 147:3, James 5:14-15
3. Pray for healing: Make it a habit to pray for God's healing, according to His sovereign will in your life.
4. Seek support: Reach out to other women of faith who can walk alongside you in your journey toward healing.

It's important to recognize that not everyone experiences certain healing on earth. Some may carry their ailments and struggles throughout their lifetime. However, this does not mean they are not healed. In eternity, in the presence of our Savior, every believer will be made whole, healed, and complete. The Apostle Paul reminds us in 1 Corinthians 15:42-44,50-55 that our earthly bodies are sown in weakness and dishonor, but they will be raised in glory and power. Our ultimate healing is not confined to our earthly existence but reaches its fulfillment in eternity, where we will be fully restored in Christ. Remember, that healing is not only an earthly experience, but also an eternal promise.

By embracing God's healing and understanding the influence of the world, our thoughts, and the devil's deceit, we can move forward in our lives with renewed strength, hope, and joy, knowing that we are truly healed in Him. May our lives be a testimony to the healing power of God's love, and may we stand firm in our belief that through Christ, " I am healed".

Chapter 3 - I am Healed
Group/Individual Questions

What does healing look like to you?

Can you share a personal experience of God's healing in your life?

How has God's healing power transformed your life?

What steps can you take to facilitate God's healing in your life?

How can you be a vessel of God's healing to others?

Chapter 4 - I am Called

Embarking on the journey to discover our calling in life can be both exhilarating and intimidating. As women of faith, we may find ourselves pondering our purpose and seeking to understand the unique plan that God has designed for each of us. The beauty of this journey lies in the knowledge that we are called by God for a specific purpose, and we can trust that He will guide us every step of the way.

Ephesians 2:10 reminds us, "For we are His workmanship, created in Christ Jesus for good works, which God prepared beforehand that we should walk in them." This verse emphasizes that God has intentionally crafted us for a purpose and has prepared good works for us to accomplish in His name.

Throughout the Bible, we encounter numerous women who were called by God to fulfill a specific purpose. Women like Esther, a young Jewish woman who became the queen of Persia and used her position to save her people from destruction. Her story is a powerful testament to the fact that God can use anyone, regardless of their background or circumstances, to carry out His purposes.

As we seek to discover and embrace our calling, it is crucial to remain mindful of the various influences that may shape our understanding of our purpose. Let's explore how "what the world says," "what we tell ourselves," and "what the devil says" can impact our journey and how we can combat these influences:

What the world says: Society often encourages us to chase after success, prestige, and material wealth as indicators of a meaningful life. However, our true calling in Christ is to serve God and others, using our gifts to further His kingdom. As we discern our calling, we must resist the temptation to conform to the world's standards and instead seek God's guidance and wisdom.

What we tell ourselves: Our own thoughts can sometimes cloud our ability to discern God's calling on our lives. We may doubt our worthiness, abilities, or readiness to answer His call. To counteract these thoughts, we must remind ourselves of the truth found in Scripture, such as Jeremiah 29:11: "For I know the plans I have for you, declares the Lord, plans to prosper you and not to harm you, plans to give you hope and a future."

What the devil says: The devil seeks to instill fear, doubt, and confusion in our hearts as we pursue our calling. He may try to convince us that we are not capable or that our efforts are futile. To combat these lies, we must stand firm in our faith and trust in God's promises, remembering that He has equipped and called us for a purpose.

As we strive to discern and embrace our calling, consider these practical steps:

1. Pray for guidance: Regularly seek God's guidance in prayer, asking Him to reveal His purpose for your life and to provide you with the wisdom and courage to pursue it.

2. Study Scripture: Dive into the Bible and explore the stories of men and women who were called by God. Reflect on their experiences and consider how God might be calling you in a similar or unique way. Abraham: Genesis 12:1-3, Moses: Exodus 3:10, Samuel: 1 Samuel 3:10, Isaiah: Isaiah 6:8, Jeremiah: Jeremiah 1:5, Mary: Luke 1:30-31, The Disciples: Matthew 4:18-20, Paul: Acts 9:15-16

3. Assess your gifts and passions: Take time to identify your natural talents, spiritual gifts, and passions. Consider how these abilities might be used to serve God and others.

4. Seek wise counsel: Consult with trusted friends, family members, or spiritual mentors who can offer insight and guidance as you discern your calling. They may be able to see your gifts and potential in ways that you might not recognize on your own.

5. Be open to new opportunities: As you explore your calling, be willing to step outside of your comfort zone and embrace new opportunities to serve and grow. God may use unexpected experiences to refine and shape your purpose.

By pursuing our calling in God, we can experience a profound sense of fulfillment and joy in knowing that we are living out the purpose for which we were created. By trusting in His guidance and stepping out in faith, we can boldly declare, "I am called."

Remember that our journey to discover our calling is a dynamic and ongoing process. As we grow and mature in our faith, our understanding of our purpose may evolve and expand. It is essential to remain flexible and adaptable, trusting that God will continue to reveal His plan for our lives as we walk with Him.

Let's strive to support and encourage one another on this journey to fulfill our God-given purpose. Share your experiences, dreams, and aspirations with fellow believers, and offer a listening ear and a helping hand to those who are also seeking their calling. Together, we can strengthen and uplift one another, ensuring that we are all moving forward in the knowledge and confidence of God's plan for our lives.

Finally, discovering and embracing our calling is a beautiful and empowering aspect of our walk with God. As we navigate the challenges and uncertainties that may arise, let us remain grounded in the truth of Scripture and the knowledge that we are called by God for a specific purpose. With faith, courage, and perseverance, we can pursue our God-given calling and experience the abundant life that He has promised to those who follow Him.

Chapter 4 - I Am Called

Group/Individual Questions

How do you understand your calling in life?

Can you share a time when you felt a strong sense of God's calling?

How are you actively pursuing your God-given calling?

What challenges have you faced in pursuing your calling, and how have you overcome them?

How can you encourage others to discover and fulfill their God-given calling?

Chapter 5 - I am Free

The feeling of being truly free is something many of us want, especially when weighed down by guilt, shame, and the burden of past mistakes. These emotions can hold us captive, preventing us from living the abundant life that God desires for us. Fortunately, as women of faith, we can find true freedom in Christ, who has already paid the price for our sins and set us free.

In John 8:36, Jesus proclaims, "So if the Son sets you free, you will be free indeed." This powerful statement reminds us that our freedom is not earned or deserved, but is a gift from God, made possible through Jesus' sacrifice on the cross.

One biblical account that beautifully illustrates the concept of freedom is the story of the woman caught in adultery, found in John 8:1-11. When the religious leaders bring her before Jesus and demand that she be stoned according to the law, Jesus responds with wisdom and grace, saying, "Let him who is without sin among you be the first to throw a stone at her." As her accusers leave one by one, Jesus offers the woman forgiveness and freedom from her past, setting her free to live a new life in Him.

To experience the freedom that Christ offers, we must first acknowledge our need for His forgiveness and grace. We must also be willing to let go of our past mistakes and embrace the new life that He has prepared for us.

In the journey to experience freedom in Christ, it is essential to understand the perspectives that shape our self-perception and beliefs.

What the world says: The world may tell us that our worth is based on our achievements, appearance, or relationships. It can also lead us to believe that we are defined by our mistakes and that we will never be truly free.

What we tell ourselves: Sometimes, we are our own worst critics, and we may tell ourselves that we are undeserving of forgiveness, love, or freedom. We must become self-aware of our internal dialogue, our self-talk, and challenge it if it's not edifying and doesn't align with the Word.

What the devil says: The deceptive voice of the enemy seeks to condemn us, magnify our flaws, and keep us trapped in guilt and shame. In our self talk, the devil's tone of voice is judgy and harsh. Remember that the Holy Spirit will convict you of your sin which may cause you to feel guilty, but condemnation is not from Him, that's the devil.

To counteract these voices and embrace our freedom in Christ, consider these practical steps:

1. Confess and repent: Be honest with God about your sins, mistakes, and areas of struggle. Ask for His forgiveness and commit to turning away from these behaviors and attitudes. If you can't think of a sin, pray like David did in Psalm 139:23-24 and ask God to search your heart and see if there is any offensive way in you.

2. Receive God's forgiveness: Accept the gift of forgiveness that God offers through Jesus Christ, trusting that your sins have been washed away and that you are a new creation in Him (2 Corinthians 5:17).

3. Let go of guilt and shame: Recognize that, as a forgiven child of God, you are no longer defined by your past mistakes. Choose to let go of guilt and shame, and embrace the freedom that comes from being forgiven (Psalm 34:5, Acts 13:38-39).

4. Forgive yourself: Practice self-forgiveness by extending the same grace and mercy to yourself that God has given you. Remember that you are not perfect, but you are deeply loved and forgiven by your Heavenly Father.

5. Walk in freedom: Live your life in the freedom that Christ has provided, making choices that reflect your new identity as a forgiven and redeemed child of God. Seek to honor Him in all

that you do and allow His Spirit to guide and empower you as you walk in freedom and forgive others.

As we embrace the freedom that is ours in Christ, we can experience the joy and peace that comes from knowing that we are no longer bound by our past mistakes or the expectations of others. With our hearts filled with gratitude, we can confidently declare, "I am free."

Chapter 5 - I Am Free

Group/Individual Questions

What does freedom mean to you in your spiritual journey?

Can you share a moment when you truly felt the freedom that comes from God?

How has embracing God's freedom changed your perspective on life?

What steps can you take to live in the freedom that God offers?

How can you help others experience the freedom that is in Christ?

Chapter 6 - I am Loved

In today's world, the definition of love has been distorted and often reduced to mere feelings or superficial attractions. Our upbringing and how our parents modeled to us the concept of love, also have a great impact on how we define and view love.

Some may have been raised in a household where affection and warmth were rare, replaced instead by strict rules and punishments. Others grew up in an environment where harsh discipline or abuse was "normal," leaving lasting impacts on our mental health and relationships, even with God.

In others, love might have been used as a bargaining tool, given only when certain conditions were met or taken away as a form of control. This confusing and often painful experience has left lasting impacts on our mental health and relationships. It can lead to struggles with self-worth, anxiety, and difficulty in forming trusting and loving relationships with others.

Even our relationship with God can be affected, as we may project these early experiences of "love" onto our understanding of God's unconditional love for us. Healing from these wounds and learning to recognize and accept true love, especially the unwavering love of God, can be a profound and transformative journey. The Bible provides a clear definition of what love truly is in 1 Corinthians 13:4-7,

"Love is patient, love is kind. It does not envy, it does not boast, it is not proud. It does not dishonor others, it is not self-seeking, it is not easily angered, it keeps no record of wrongs."

It is vital to remember that God's love for us is unchanging and everlasting. No matter what we face, whether it be personal struggles, heartbreak, or loss, we can find comfort in the truth that God's love for us is unwavering.

Romans 8:38-39 states, "For I am convinced that neither death nor life, neither angels nor demons, neither the present nor the future, nor any powers, neither height nor depth, nor anything else in all creation, will be able to separate us from the love of God that is in Christ Jesus our Lord." These powerful words assure us that there is absolutely nothing that can separate us from God's love.

What the world says: The world often equates love with physical attraction, material wealth, or fleeting emotions. True love, as described in 1 Corinthians 13, is selfless, enduring, and unconditional.

What we tell ourselves: Our past experiences and inner critic may lead us to believe that we are unlovable or unworthy of God's love. We must counter these thoughts with the truth of God's Word, such as Romans 5:8, "But God demonstrates His own love for us in this: While we were still sinners, Christ died for us."

What the devil says: The devil seeks to distort our understanding of love and make us doubt God's love for us. We must resist these lies with the truth found in Scripture, such as 1 John 4:16, "And so we know and rely on the love God has for us. God is love."

A beautiful example of God's love can be found in the story of the Samaritan woman at the well, as described in John 4:4-26. In this account, Jesus does something extraordinary by breaking societal norms and engaging in conversation with a Samaritan woman. At that time, Jews and Samaritans had deep-seated animosities, and it was highly unusual for a Jewish man to speak to a Samaritan woman, especially in public. Yet, Jesus approached her with compassion and dignity, offering her "living water."

The woman was astonished by Jesus' request for a drink and his knowledge of her past, including her multiple marriages and current living situation. Despite her past and the judgment she faced from her community, Jesus did not condemn her. Instead, He offered her love, acceptance, and eternal life. He revealed Himself as the Messiah, the one who could quench her spiritual thirst and provide a love that transcends all human understanding.

To embrace our identity as loved by God, we must first accept the depth and magnitude of His love for us, as demonstrated in this story. This means letting go of any doubts or fears that tell us we are unworthy or unlovable and choosing to believe God's promises of love and acceptance. The encounter with the Samaritan woman is a powerful reminder that God's love is not limited by our past mistakes, societal judgments, or personal feelings of inadequacy. His love reaches out to us, offering forgiveness, healing, and a new beginning. It's a love that sees beyond our flaws and embraces us as we are, inviting us into a relationship with Him that is both transformative and eternal

Here are some practical steps to help you embrace your identity as loved by God:

1. Reflect on Scripture: Spend time meditating on Bible verses like Romans 8:38-39, 1 Corinthians 13:4-7, and 1 John 4:16.
2. Pray for a deeper understanding of God's love: Ask God to open your heart to His love, and heal from any past distortion of love.
3. Surround yourself with reminders of God's love: Place visual reminders of God's love in your space.
4. Share God's love with others: Extend God's love to others through your actions and words.

Remember, as you learn to embrace your identity as loved by God, it is essential to continually reassess the messages you receive from the world, your own thoughts, and the enemy's lies. Be vigilant in guarding your heart and mind against anything that contradicts the truth of God's love.

As we walk in the confidence of knowing we are loved by God, our lives will be transformed, our relationships will be enriched, and our hearts will overflow with gratitude and joy. Let us boldly proclaim, "I am loved."

Chapter 6 - I Am Loved

Group/Individual Questions

How do you personally experience God's love?

Can you share a time when you felt deeply loved by God?

How does knowing that you are loved by God affect your relationships with others?

What can you do to remind yourself of God's love in difficult times?

How can you express God's love to others in your life?

Chapter 7 - I am Accepted

Acceptance is a fundamental human need, deeply intertwined with our mental and emotional well-being. In a world that often judges us by superficial standards, the quest for acceptance can become a source of anxiety and depression. The pressure to conform to societal norms, whether in appearance, behavior, or success, can lead to feelings of inadequacy and rejection. From a mental health perspective, the lack of acceptance, both from others and ourselves, can destroy self-esteem and create feelings of isolation.

In contrast, acceptance by others fosters a sense of belonging and validation, while self-acceptance is a cornerstone of mental resilience. It empowers us to embrace our uniqueness without the constant fear of judgment. In God's kingdom, understanding and accepting God's unconditional love is a profound source of healing, and foundation of how to view acceptance.

The pursuit of pleasing others can become a dangerous trap, leading us away from our authentic selves and God's unique purpose for our lives. People-pleasing often stems from a fear of rejection or a desire for approval, but it can result in a loss of identity and integrity. We may find ourselves compromising our values, neglecting our needs, and living in constant anxiety about others' opinions. This path is not only exhausting but also unfulfilling, as it is impossible to please everyone. The Bible reminds us that our primary focus should be on pleasing God, not people. Hebrews 11:6 states, "Without faith, it is impossible to please God." Our faith in God and obedience to His will are what truly matter. When we seek to please God above all else, we find freedom, purpose, and true acceptance.

What the world says: The world tells us that acceptance is contingent upon conformity - that we must be perfect in our appearance, career, and relationships to be accepted. These external standards can leave us feeling unlovable and unworthy.

What we tell ourselves: We often tell ourselves that we are undeserving of such love and acceptance. Our inner critic amplifies our flaws and mistakes, making us doubt our worthiness of God's unconditional love.

What the devil says: The devil also tries to deceive us, whispering lies that we are beyond redemption and that God's love cannot reach us. He wants to keep us trapped in a cycle of self-doubt and fear, preventing us from embracing our identity in Christ.

Despite these negative influences, through Christ, we can find the unconditional love and belonging our hearts yearn for. God accepts us, flaws, imperfections, and past mistakes included.

A poignant example of this acceptance is found in the story of an unnamed sinful woman who anoints Jesus' feet with perfume and her tears, then wipes them with her hair (Luke 7:36-50). While dining at the house of Simon the Pharisee, Jesus is approached by this woman, who expresses her love and repentance in this intimate act. Simon criticizes Jesus for allowing such a sinful woman to touch Him, but Jesus responds with a parable that illustrates the depth of the woman's love and the forgiveness she has received. He accepts her, not for her perfection but for her faith, contrasting sharply with Simon's judgment and rejection.

Ephesians 1:4-6 states, "For He chose us in Him before the creation of the world to be holy and blameless in His sight. In love, He predestined us for adoption to sonship through Jesus Christ, in accordance with His pleasure and will—to the praise of His glorious grace, which He has freely given us in the One He loves." This passage highlights that God's acceptance is not based on our accomplishments but on His love and grace, freely given through Christ.

Practical steps to embrace acceptance:

1. Reflect on Scripture: Meditate on Bible verses that affirm God's acceptance and love for you. Allow these truths to solidify your worth and value in God's eyes, drowning out the noise from the world, your own thoughts, and the devil's deception. Ephesians 1:6, Romans 15:7, 1 Corinthians 6:11, John 1:12, Romans 8:15, Galatians 3:26, Colossians 1:21-22, 1 Peter 2:9, 2 Corinthians 5:17
2. Pray for a deeper understanding of God's acceptance: Ask God to help you grasp the fullness of His love and acceptance and

guide you in letting go of the need for others' approval and the lies you tell yourself.

3. Surround yourself with supportive and affirming relationships: Seek out friendships and communities that encourage and uplift you in your faith, helping you grow in your understanding of God's love and acceptance.

4. Extend acceptance to others: As you experience God's acceptance in your life, be intentional about extending that same acceptance to others, countering the messages they receive from the world, the devil, or their own self-doubt.

5. Practice self-acceptance: Appreciate your unique qualities, gifts, and experiences, recognizing that you are a beloved and accepted child of God. Treat yourself with kindness and compassion, knowing that you are worthy of love and acceptance. If you are having a hard time accepting who you are, it doesn't mean it's all of you. It could be an area that God is convicting you and working on. While it is "come as you are" , you shouldn't "stay as you are" if you are following Christ daily.

As we embrace our identity as accepted by God, we can experience the freedom and peace that come from knowing we belong to Him and are deeply loved and valued. With hearts full of gratitude, let us confidently declare, "I am accepted."

Chapter 7 - I Am Accepted

Group/Individual Questions

What does it mean to you to be accepted by God?

Can you share a time when you felt God's acceptance in a powerful way?

How has knowing that you are accepted by God changed your self-image?

What can you do to live in the reality of God's acceptance?

How can you show God's acceptance to others?

Chapter 8 - I am Chosen

When popularity, status, and the approval of others come into play, it can be easy to feel overlooked or undervalued. However, we can find comfort and confidence in the truth that God has chosen us – not because of our accomplishments or abilities but simply because of His great love for us.

1 Peter 2:9 says, "But you are a chosen people, a royal priesthood, a holy nation, God's special possession, that you may declare the praises of Him who called you out of darkness into His wonderful light." This verse reminds us that our identity as chosen by God is not based on anything we have done or earned but is solely the result of His grace and love.

The story of Rahab, a woman living in the city of Jericho, is a powerful example of God's divine choosing. Despite her profession as a prostitute and her status as an outsider, God chose Rahab to play a crucial role in the Israelites' conquest of the Promised Land. Her faith and courage in hiding the Israelite spies not only saved her own life and the lives of her family members but also secured her place in the lineage of Jesus Christ (Matthew 1:5).

To embrace our identity as chosen by God, we must first recognize that our worth and value come from Him alone. We must also be willing to trust in His plan and purpose for our lives, even when we may not fully understand it.

However, we are often bombarded with messages that can distort our understanding of our chosen identity in Christ. These messages come from the world, our own self-talk, and the lies the devil may try to deceive us with.

What the world says: Society often tells us that we must achieve certain milestones, acquire material possessions, or attain specific social statuses to be considered worthy or valuable. It can be easy to feel unchosen or left behind if we don't conform to these expectations.

What we tell ourselves: Sometimes, our own negative self-talk can undermine our belief in our chosen identity. We may criticize ourselves for our shortcomings, doubting that we are truly chosen by God.

What the devil says: The enemy may try to sow seeds of doubt in our minds, whispering lies that we are not chosen or loved by God, attempting to distance us from our true identity in Christ.

In light of these challenges, here are some practical steps to help you embrace your identity as chosen by God:

1. Reflect on Scripture: Meditate on Bible verses that speak of God's choosing and purpose for your life. Allow these truths to counteract the false messages you receive from the world, yourself, and the devil. Jeremiah 1:5, Ephesians 1:4-5, Ephesians

2:10, Romans 8:28, 1 Peter 2:9, 2 Timothy 1:9, Isaiah 43:7, John 15:16

2. Pray for guidance and discernment: Ask God to reveal His plan and purpose for your life and to help you walk in the path He has chosen for you. Pray for the wisdom to discern the lies of the enemy and the courage to reject them (James 1:5).

3. Surround yourself with supportive and encouraging relationships: Cultivate friendships and community with other believers who will uplift and encourage you in your journey of faith, reminding you of your chosen identity in Christ.

4. Embrace your unique gifts and abilities: Recognize and celebrate the unique gifts and talents that God has given you, using them to serve others and bring glory to His name.

5. Share your story: As you grow in your understanding of your chosen identity in Christ, look for opportunities to share your testimony with others. Your story of God's choosing and purpose can be an inspiration and encouragement to those who may be struggling to find their own sense of belonging and purpose.

As we embrace our identity as chosen by God, we can experience the peace and joy that come from knowing that we are chosen by our Creator.

Chapter 8 - I am Chosen

Group/Individual Questions

What does it mean to you to be chosen by God?

Can you share a time when you felt a strong sense of being chosen by God?

How has knowing that you are chosen by God affected your life?

What can you do to remind yourself that you are chosen by God?

How can you help others understand that they are chosen by God?

Chapter 9 - I am Content

Do you ever feel like finding contentment seems like an elusive goal? We're constantly bombarded by messages telling us that we need more, that we're not enough, or that true happiness lies just around the corner.

What the world says: Marketing, other people, social media, can influence us to believe we are always in need of more, pushing us into a constant state of dissatisfaction.

What we tell ourselves: We tell ourselves that we need a bigger house, a better job, or more money to feel content. But these things can never truly satisfy us, because true contentment is not dependent on our external circumstances.

What the devil says: The devil also plays a role in our discontentment, whispering lies to us that we are not good enough or that we need more to be happy. He tries to deceive us into believing that our worth is based on our possessions or achievements, rather than on our identity as children of God.

Let's explore what it means to be content in God and how we can nurture a sense of contentment that is grounded in our faith. The Bible teaches us that true contentment comes from a deep and abiding relationship with God. In Philippians 4:11-13, the Apostle Paul writes: "Not that I speak in regard to need, for I have learned in whatever state I am, to be content: I know how to be abased, and I know how to abound. Everywhere and in all things, I have learned both to be full and to be hungry, both to abound and to suffer need. I can do all things through Christ who strengthens me."

Paul's words remind us that contentment is not dependent on our circumstances, but rather on our relationship with God. When we place our trust in Him and rely on His strength, we can find contentment in any situation, whether we are experiencing abundance or hardship.

One example of contentment in the Bible is the story of Mary and Martha, found in Luke 10:38-42. Martha was busy with preparations, while Mary chose to sit at Jesus' feet and listen to His teaching. Although Martha was frustrated with her sister's apparent lack of involvement, Jesus gently reminded her that Mary had chosen what was truly important – spending time in His presence.

Contentment is something we all want; to be able to enjoy what we have, to feel like we have enough, to feel satisfied. It's something that doesn't come naturally. To cultivate contentment in our lives, we must learn to prioritize our relationship with God and focus on the things that truly matter. This involves letting go of the need to constantly strive for more and instead finding satisfaction in God's provision and grace.

Here are some practical steps you can take to nurture contentment in your life:

1. Reflect on what the world, yourself, and the devil says: Be aware of the messages that are bombarding you from different sources and recognize their lies. Know the difference from what God's word says versus everyone else.

2. Spend time with God: Make it a priority to spend time each day in prayer, Scripture reading, and quiet reflection. As you draw closer to God, you will begin to find contentment in His presence. Ask God to give you contentment with what you've worked hard to obtain (Ecclesiastes 3:12-13).

3. Practice gratitude: Cultivate an attitude of gratitude by intentionally focusing on the blessings in your life such answered prayers, goals achieved, relationships. Keep a gratitude journal or a notes list on your phone. You can also share your gratitude with others as a way to remind yourself of God's goodness and provision and it also encourages the other person.

4. Let go of comparisons: Resist the temptation to compare yourself to others, as this can easily lead to feelings of discontentment. Instead, focus on your unique gifts, talents, and blessings, and celebrate the person God has created you to be.

5. Simplify your life: Evaluate your priorities and consider simplifying your life to make more room. Another key to

nurturing contentment is to learn to manage our thoughts and emotions. As women, we often experience a range of emotions throughout the day, from joy and excitement to sadness and frustration. Learning to recognize and manage these emotions in a healthy way can help us maintain a sense of contentment and balance.

One way to manage our thoughts and emotions is through mindfulness. Mindfulness involves being fully present in the moment and observing our thoughts and emotions without judgment. By practicing mindfulness, we can learn to accept our feelings without being overwhelmed by them, and we can develop a greater sense of inner peace and contentment.

Another important aspect of managing our thoughts and emotions is learning to take our thoughts captive. In 2 Corinthians 10:5, the Apostle Paul writes: "We demolish arguments and every pretension that sets itself up against the knowledge of God, and we take captive every thought to make it obedient to Christ." This means that when negative or harmful thoughts enter our minds, we can choose to reject them and instead focus on the truth of God's word.

To cultivate contentment in our lives, we must also learn to let go of the things that are beyond our control. This involves trusting in God's plan and sovereignty, even when we don't understand it. As Proverbs 3:5-6 says, "Trust in the Lord with all your heart and lean not on your own understanding; in all your ways submit to him, and he will make your paths straight."

Finally, we must recognize that contentment is not a destination but a journey. It is something that we must continually cultivate and nurture throughout our lives. As we draw closer to God and learn to manage our thoughts and emotions in a healthy way, we will find that contentment becomes a natural part of who we are.

Cultivating contentment is an essential part of our journey as women of faith. By prioritizing our relationship with God, managing our thoughts and emotions, letting go of what we can't control, and recognizing that contentment is a daily habit, we can find true satisfaction and joy in our lives. As we seek contentment in God, we can confidently declare, "I am content."

Chapter 9 - I Am Content

Group/Individual Questions

What does contentment mean to you in your spiritual journey?

Can you share a moment when you truly felt content in God's
provision or lack thereof?

How has embracing God's provision changed your perspective on life?

What steps can you take to live in the contentment that God offers?

How can you help others experience the contentment that is in Christ?

Chapter 10 - I am Courageous

Courage. It's a word we hear often, but what does it really mean? And why does it seem so hard to grasp? Maybe you've faced situations that left you feeling scared or overwhelmed. Perhaps you've been held back by past traumas, anxiety, or the fear of failure. You're not alone. Many of us struggle with these feelings, but here's the good news: courage is not something we have to muster up on our own. It's not about being fearless or invincible. True courage is about stepping out in faith, even when we feel weak, trusting that God's strength will carry us through.

What the world says: "Be safe. Avoid risks. Protect yourself. Don't speak up, stay quiet." The world often equates courage with recklessness, urging us to play it safe and avoid taking risks. This mindset can lead to a life of limitations and missed opportunities. We must recognize that true courage is not about recklessness but about stepping out in faith, trusting in God's guidance and strength.

What we tell ourselves: "I'm not strong enough. I can't handle this. It's too much." Our inner critic may fill our minds with doubts and fears, making us feel inadequate and overwhelmed. These thoughts can paralyze us and prevent us from pursuing our dreams and calling. We must replace these lies with the truth of God's Word, such as Philippians 4:13, "I can do all things through Christ who strengthens me."

What the devil says: "You're a coward. You're not capable. You're going to fail." The devil seeks to undermine our confidence and make us doubt our abilities. He wants us to feel defeated and powerless. We must resist these lies with the truth found in Scripture, such as Joshua 1:9, "Be strong and courageous. Do not be afraid; do not be discouraged, for the Lord your God will be with you wherever you go."

One of the most inspiring examples of courage in the Bible is the story of Deborah, a prophetess and judge of Israel. During a time when Israel was oppressed by a Canaanite king, Deborah courageously led the Israelite army into battle, trusting in God's guidance and deliverance (Judges 4-5).

Deborah's story is not just a historical account; it's a relatable example for all of us. She was a woman in a male-dominated society, called by God to lead and make a difference. Her courage was not born out of her own strength but from her faith in God.

Like Deborah, we may face situations that seem insurmountable. We may feel outnumbered, overwhelmed, or out of our depth. But Deborah's story reminds us that with God, all things are possible. Her faith and courage not only secured victory for her people but also served as an inspiration for generations to come.

Her story challenges us to step out in faith, to trust in God's guidance, and to embrace the courage that comes from knowing that He is with us. It's a reminder that our courage is not limited by our circumstances, our gender, our background, or our abilities. With God, we can overcome any obstacle and achieve great things.

To embrace our identity as courageous, we must first recognize the lies that the world, ourselves, and the devil try to tell us. We must then turn to God's truth and allow His presence and power to fill us with courage.

Here are some practical steps to help you embrace your identity as courageous:

1. Reflect on Scripture: Meditate on Bible verses that speak of God's presence and courage. Allow these truths to encourage you and build your faith in His ability to sustain and support you. Spending time with Jesus makes us courageous, see Acts 4:13. Joshua 1:9, Deuteronomy 31:6, Psalm 23:4, Isaiah 41:10, 2 Timothy 1:7, 1 Corinthians 16:13, Psalm 27:1, Psalm 31:24, Philippians 4:13

2. Pray for courage: Regularly ask God to fill you with courage and faith, especially during times of fear or uncertainty. Trust that He is faithful to provide the courage you need when you need it most.

3. Surround yourself with supportive and uplifting relationships: Cultivate friendships and community with other believers who will encourage you in your faith, and help pray for you to be courageous.

4. Face your fears: Identify areas of your life where fear is holding you back, and take practical steps to face those fears with God's help. This may involve seeking counsel, prayer, or simply taking a leap of faith.

5. Share your story: As you experience God's courage in your own life, encourage others in their faith and walk with God by sharing how God has helped you face your fears and given you courage.

As we embrace our identity as courageous, we can face each day with confidence, knowing that we are not alone in our struggles. With faith in God's presence and support, let us boldly declare, "I am courageous."

Chapter 10 - I Am Courageous

Group/Individual Questions

How do you personally experience God's courage?

Can you share a time when you felt deeply courageous because of God?

How does knowing that you are courageous with God affect your relationships with others?

What can you do to remind yourself of God's courage in difficult times?

How can you express God's courage to others in your life?

Chapter 11 - I am Beautiful

When we place undue importance on outward appearance and superficial beauty, it can be challenging for us to see our true worth and beauty. However, we are called to embrace a different kind of beauty – one that is rooted in our identity as children of God and reflects His love and grace.

What the world says: The world tells us that our worth and beauty are determined by our physical appearance, the clothes we wear, and the status we hold in society. It can be easy to fall into the trap of believing that our value is based on these external factors.

What we tell ourselves: We may tell ourselves that we are not beautiful enough, that we need to change our appearance to fit in or be accepted, or that we will never measure up to the world's standards of beauty. These negative self-talk patterns can damage our self-esteem and lead us away from embracing our true beauty.

What the devil says: The devil seeks to undermine our confidence in God's love and our identity as beautiful and beloved children of God. He may tempt us to compare ourselves to others or believe lies about our worth and value. However, we can resist his attacks by renewing our minds with the truth of God's Word.

1 Peter 3:3-4 says, "Your beauty should not come from outward adornment, such as elaborate hairstyles and the wearing of gold jewelry

or fine clothes. Rather, it should be that of your inner self, the unfading beauty of a gentle and quiet spirit, which is of great worth in God's sight." This verse reminds us that true beauty is found within and is cultivated through a growing relationship with our Heavenly Father.

The story of Hannah, the mother of the prophet Samuel, is a powerful example of inner beauty. Despite facing the pain of infertility and ridicule from her husband's other wife, Hannah persevered in her faith, earnestly praying to the Lord for a child. In doing so, she displayed a beauty that went beyond her physical appearance, showing her deep faith, resilience, and humility (1 Samuel 1).

To embrace our identity as beautiful, we must first recognize that our true beauty comes from God and is reflected in the qualities of our heart and spirit.

Here are some practical steps to help you embrace your identity as beautiful:

1. Reflect on Scripture: Meditate on Bible verses that speak of God's love and the beauty He sees within us. Allow these truths to reshape your understanding of beauty and self-worth. Proverbs 31:30, Ephesians 2:4-5, Psalm 139:14, Song of Solomon 4:7, Romans 5:8, Zephaniah 3:17, 1 Peter 3:3-4, Jeremiah 31:3, Romans 8:38-39

2. Pray for inner beauty: Ask God to help you have a humble spirit and trust that He is faithful to transform you from the inside out. Pray that God help you become a Proverbs 31:30 woman, "Charm is deceptive, and beauty does not last; but a woman who fears the LORD will be greatly praised." Fear in biblical context refers to respecting God, worshiping Him in awe, and trusting Him wholeheartedly.

3. Surround yourself with supportive and uplifting relationships: Cultivate friendships and community with other believers that encourage you to be embrace your God given beauty, your uniqueness, and your authentic self.

4. Share your story: Your story of inner transformation can be an inspiration and encouragement to those who may be struggling with their own self-image.

As we embrace our identity as beautiful, we can live confidently in the knowledge that our true beauty is found in our relationship with God. With gratitude for the unfading beauty He has placed within us, let us joyfully declare, "I am beautiful".

Chapter 11 - I Am Beautiful

Group/Individual Questions

What does it mean to you to be seen as beautiful by God?

Can you share a time when you felt God's affirmation of your beauty in a powerful way?

How has knowing that you are beautiful in God's eyes changed your self-image?

What can you do to live in the reality of God's affirmation of your beauty?

How can you show others that they are beautiful in God's eyes?

Chapter 12 - I am Strong

As women, we often find ourselves struggling to balance the many demands and responsibilities of our lives. We may feel overwhelmed, exhausted, and inadequate at times. But the truth is, our strength doesn't come from ourselves; it comes from God, who equips and empowers us for every situation.

What the world says: The world tells us that strength is found in our own abilities and accomplishments. We're encouraged to push ourselves to the limit and prove our worth through our achievements.

What we tell ourselves: We often believe that we have to do it all and be everything to everyone. We put immense pressure on ourselves to be perfect and to never show weakness or vulnerability.

What the devil says: The devil tries to convince us that we're not strong enough, that we're not capable of handling the challenges we face. He wants us to doubt our ability to trust in God and rely on His strength.

Isaiah 40:31 serves as a beacon of hope and a potent reminder of God's unending strength. The verse reads, "But those who hope in the Lord will renew their strength. They will soar on wings like eagles; they will run and not grow weary, they will walk and not be weary." This verse is a testament to the transformative power of faith in God.

The imagery of soaring on wings like eagles is particularly compelling. Eagles are known for their strength and endurance, capable of soaring to great heights and weathering powerful storms. This metaphor serves to illustrate that with faith in God, we too can rise above our challenges and hardships, no matter how formidable they may seem. We can run the race of life without growing weary, and we can walk through the trials and tribulations of life without losing heart. This is not because of our own strength, but because of the strength that God provides. It's a strength that is not merely physical but also spiritual and emotional, enabling us to persevere through life's most challenging circumstances.

The Widow of Zarephath, from the Old Testament (1 Kings 17:8-24 ESV), is a remarkable example of a woman who demonstrated extraordinary strength through her trust in God. Despite facing famine and having only enough food for one last meal, she chose to obey the prophet Elijah's request to feed him first. Her obedience and trust in God's word through the prophet, led to a miraculous provision where her jar of flour and jug of oil never ran out. This story is a testament to the strength that comes from trusting in God's provision, even in the face of scarcity and uncertainty.

In both Isaiah 40:31 and the story of The Widow of Zarephath, we see the theme of strength in God being beautifully portrayed. These biblical accounts invite us to lean on God's strength, to trust in

His provision, and to find comfort in His protection. They remind us that our strength does not come from our own abilities or achievements, but from our relationship with God, who is our ever-present help in times of need.

To embrace our identity as strong in God, we must first acknowledge our own weaknesses and limitations, allowing God to be our source of strength and power. In doing so, we can face life's challenges with confidence, knowing that He is with us every step of the way.

Here are some practical steps to help you embrace your strength in God:

1. Reflect on Scripture: Meditate on Bible verses that speak to God's strength and power. Allow these truths to remind you of His ability to strengthen and sustain you in times of difficulty. Isaiah 40:31, Philippians 4:13, 2 Corinthians 12:9-10, Psalm 46:1, Ephesians 6:10, Psalm 28:7, Exodus 15:2, 1 Chronicles 16:11, Habakkuk 3:19, Nehemiah 8:10

2. Pray for strength: When faced with challenges or difficult circumstances, turn to God in prayer, asking for His strength and guidance to help you navigate each situation. Ask God in the areas that you are weak…may he be strong! 2 Corinthians 12:9

3. Share your struggles: Reach out to trusted friends, family members, or spiritual mentors who can offer support,

encouragement, and prayer as you face life's challenges. Remember, you are not alone.

4. Encourage others: As you experience God's strength in your own life, look for opportunities to share your journey with others who may be struggling. Offer words of encouragement, hope, and inspiration, pointing them to the source of our strength - God.

As we learn to rely on God's strength rather than our own, we can experience a newfound sense of resilience and perseverance in the face of life's challenges. Let us walk boldly in our faith, knowing that, through Christ, we can declare, "I am strong."

Chapter 12 - I Am Strong

Group/Individual Questions

What does it mean to you to be strong in God?

Can you share a time when you felt a strong sense of God's strength in your life?

How has knowing that you are strong in God affected your life?

What can you do to remind yourself that you are strong in God?

How can you help others understand that they are strong in God?

Chapter 13 - I am Empowered

We often face obstacles and challenges that can make us feel powerless or inadequate. However, as women of faith, we know that our true power comes from God. When we understand and embrace our identity as empowered by Him, we can overcome any obstacle and live our lives to the fullest.

Romans 8:37 reminds us that "in all these things we are more than conquerors through him who loved us." This verse reminds us that through our faith in Christ, we have access to a power that is greater than anything we could ever face.

The story of Lydia, a successful businesswoman who became one of the first converts to Christianity in Europe, is a powerful example of a woman who embraced her God-given power. Lydia used her position and influence to support the early Christian church, and her home became a hub for spreading the Gospel throughout the region (Acts 16:14-15, 40).

Lydia sold purple cloth, which was a big deal back in the day. But even with all her success, she felt like something was missing. That's when she met Paul and heard about Christianity. What's more, Lydia didn't just keep her new faith to herself. She opened up her home and made it a place where other Christians could hang out, pray, and support each other. Back then, women didn't usually get to play such important roles. But Lydia did, proving that through God, everyone is valued and can make a difference.

Lydia's story is a great example for us today. Lots of us are chasing success, just like she was, as a form of having an impactful role in society. But her story reminds us that the most important thing isn't what we have or what we achieve, but our relationship with God. And just like Lydia, we can use whatever we have, whether it's our home, our money, or our time, to help others and spread God's love.

So whether you are a homeschooling mom, or a woman in business, or someone who just started college, to embrace our identity as empowered, we must first recognize that our true power comes from God and is available to us through our relationship with Him.

What the world says: The world says power comes from wealth, status, and influence. The world will tell us to do whatever it takes to obtain power including being dishonest, being manipulative, taking advantage or mistreating others.

What we tell ourselves: We may tell ourselves that we are not powerful enough to make a difference, or that we are not worthy of using our power for good. We may also tell ourselves that to be powerful requires being blunt, harsh, emotionless, and never showing vulnerability.

What the devil says: The devil will try to convince us that we are powerless, and to be powerful would involve making ungodly decisions.

Here are some practical steps to help you embrace your identity as empowered:

1. Reflect on Scripture: Meditate on Bible verses that speak of God's power and strength within us. Allow these truths to reshape your understanding of your capabilities and potential. Ephesians 3:16, Philippians 4:13, Isaiah 40:29, 2 Corinthians 12:9-10, 1 Corinthians 16:13, Ephesians 6:10, 2 Timothy 1:7, Colossians 1:11, 1 Chronicles 29:12, Zechariah 4:6

2. Pray for empowerment: Ask God to fill you with His power and strength, enabling you to face challenges and pursue your purpose with courage and confidence.

3. Surround yourself with supportive and uplifting relationships: Pursue friendships with other mature Christians that will encourage you to pray bold prayers, make godly decisions, and keep Christ in all things.

4. Pursue your purpose: Identify your unique gifts and talents, and seek opportunities to use them in service to others and to glorify God.

5. Share your story: As you start understanding how much power you have through Christ, keep an eye out for chances to share your journey with others. Your story about tackling tough times and really grabbing hold of the power God gave you can give a real boost to others who might be having a hard time feeling powerful themselves.

As we embrace our identity as empowered, we can live confidently in the knowledge that our true power is found in our relationship with God. With gratitude for the strength He has placed within us, let us boldly declare, "I am empowered."

Chapter 13 - I Am Empowered

Group/Individual Questions

What does it mean to you to be empowered by God?

Can you share a time when you felt God's empowerment in a significant way?

How has knowing that you are empowered by God changed your approach to challenges?

What can you do to live in the empowerment that God provides?

How can you encourage others to step into their God-given authority?

Chapter 14 - I am Worthy

In the hearts of many, particularly women, lies a hidden struggle with feelings of unworthiness and insecurity. These emotions often stem from societal pressures, personal failures, or the harsh judgments of others. The world's standards can lead us to believe the lies that we are not good enough or deserving of love and respect. But what if there's a different way to see ourselves?

The Bible offers a profound truth that stands in stark contrast to the world's judgments. Romans 5:8 tells us, "But God demonstrates his own love for us in this: While we were still sinners, Christ died for us." This verse is a powerful reminder that our worth is not determined by our performance or our past. God's love is unconditional, and He sees our true value, even when we fail to see it ourselves.

One of the most compelling examples of this truth is found in the life of Mary Magdalene. Often identified with a troubled past, Mary's life was transformed by the love and acceptance of Jesus. He saw her true value and called her to follow Him. She became one of His most devoted followers, and her story is a testament to the transformative power of Christ's love.

In John 20:11-18, Mary Magdalene's faithfulness is honored as she becomes the first person to witness the resurrected Christ. This significant moment underscores the special place she held among Jesus' followers.

The message of God's love and the example of Mary Magdalene are not confined to the pages of history; they have practical implications for women today. Those who struggle with feelings of unworthiness can find hope and healing in the truth that they are loved and valued by God. Embracing this truth can lead to a transformation in how we see ourselves and how we live our lives.

To fully embrace our identity as worthy, we must first recognize and reject the lies of the world, the negative self-talk that we tell ourselves, and the deception of the enemy.

What the world says: Society will say we have to earn the feeling of being worthy through productivity or performance, beauty, or talent.

What we tell ourselves: We may have the negative core belief of "I am not worthy," which may have formed from life experiences. When we don't challenge it, it becomes a lens through which we view the world, others, ourselves, and it affects how we interpret interactions.

What the devil says: The devil can remind us of our failures and tell us we are disqualified. Just remind him of his end and put on the full armor of God (Revelation 20:10, Epheisans 6:11). We must renew our minds with the truth of God's Word and cultivate a deeper understanding of His love for us. Our worth is defined by God's words.

Here are some practical steps to help you embrace your identity as worthy:

1. Recognize your worth in God's eyes: Your worth is not based on what you do, but rather on who you are as a beloved child of God. No matter what you may face in life, you can rest in the assurance that your value is unchanging and eternal.

2. Meditate on God's Word: Allow the truth of Scripture to transform your thinking and reshape your understanding of your worth and value. Memorize Bible verses that speak to your identity in Christ, and reflect on them regularly. 2 Corinthians 5:17, Galatians 2:20, Ephesians 2:10, 1 Peter 2:9, Romans 8:1, Romans 6:6, Colossians 3:3, 1 Corinthians 6:19-20, Ephesians 1:5, John 1:12, Romans 8:17, 1 John 3:1-2, Galatians 3:26-28, Colossians 2:9-10

3. Surround yourself with godly influences: Seek out relationships that will uplift and encourage you, and avoid those that tear you down or make you feel inferior.

4. Practice self-care: Take care of yourself physically, emotionally, and spiritually. Treat yourself with kindness and respect, just as God treats you with love and compassion.

5. Serve others: Serving others not only takes our focus off ourselves, but it also allows us to see our worth in action. As we use our God-given gifts to bless others, we are reminded of our value in His kingdom.

As we embrace our identity as worthy in Christ, we can experience freedom from the burden of insecurity and self-doubt. Let us boldly declare, "I am worthy".

Chapter 14 - I Am Worthy

Group/Individual Questions

What does it mean to you to be worthy in God's eyes?

Can you share a time when you felt a deep sense of your worthiness to God?

How has knowing that you are worthy in God's eyes affected your self-esteem?

What can you do to remind yourself of your worthiness in God's kingdom?

How can you help others understand their worthiness in God's eyes?

Chapter 15 - I am Resilient

Life is full of challenges and setbacks, but as women of God, we can tap into a wellspring of inner strength and resilience that comes from our identity in Christ. Resilience is the ability to bounce back from adversity and to thrive in the face of difficulties. It is a quality that is essential for a fulfilling and meaningful life, and it is something that we can cultivate through our relationship with God.

What the world says: The world often equates resilience with self-reliance and the ability to "tough it out" alone. It suggests that showing vulnerability or seeking help is a sign of weakness. However, our resilience as women of God is not about being invincible or unaffected by life's challenges. It's about leaning into God's strength, acknowledging our need for His support, and trusting in His ability to bring us through.

What the devil says: The devil seeks to undermine our resilience by magnifying our failures and setbacks. He may try to convince us that we're not strong enough, that our struggles are too great, or that God won't come through for us. But we must resist these lies and stand firm in the truth of God's Word. As Romans 8:37 assures us, "In all these things we are more than conquerors through him who loved us." We are not defeated by our challenges, but are made resilient through Christ.

What we tell ourselves: Sometimes, our own thoughts and fears can hinder our resilience. We may doubt our ability to bounce back from adversity, or we may feel overwhelmed by the magnitude of our struggles. It's crucial to replace these negative self-perceptions with the truth of who God says we are. As 2 Corinthians 12:9-10 reminds us, "But he said to me, 'My grace is sufficient for you, for my power is made perfect in weakness.' Therefore I will boast all the more gladly about my weaknesses, so that Christ's power may rest on me. That is why, for Christ's sake, I delight in weaknesses, in insults, in hardships, in persecutions, in difficulties. For when I am weak, then I am strong."

One of the greatest examples of resilience in the Bible is the story of Mary, the mother of Jesus. Mary demonstrated remarkable resilience and strength of character in the face of adversity. From the moment she was told by the angel Gabriel that she would bear the Son of God, Mary faced significant challenges.

One example of Mary's resilience is when she traveled to Bethlehem while heavily pregnant. This journey would have been physically and emotionally taxing, but Mary trusted in God's plan for her life and persevered. When she arrived in Bethlehem, she gave birth to Jesus in a humble stable, surrounded by animals and far from the comforts of home. Despite the difficult circumstances, Mary remained steadfast in her faith and trust in God.

Another example of Mary's resilience is when she witnessed the crucifixion of her son. This would have been an incredibly traumatic and heart-wrenching experience, but Mary remained strong and resolute in her faith. She stood at the foot of the cross and watched as her son suffered and died, knowing that his sacrifice would bring salvation to the world.

Mary's life is a powerful example of how we can cultivate resilience in our own lives. Here are some practical steps to help you develop resilience:

1. Trust in God's plan: Just as Mary trusted in God's plan for her life, we too can trust in His plan for ours. When we face difficult circumstances, we can find strength in the knowledge that God is with us and has a purpose for our lives.

2. Surround yourself with supportive relationships: Mary had a strong support network, including her husband Joseph, her cousin Elizabeth, and the other women who were present at Jesus' birth. We too can benefit from supportive relationships with friends, family, and members of our church community.

3. Cultivate a positive mindset: Mary remained positive and hopeful, even in the midst of difficult circumstances. We can follow her example by focusing on the good things in our lives and practicing gratitude.

4. Practice self-care: Mary would have taken care of herself and her baby during her pregnancy, and we too can prioritize self-care by taking care of our physical, emotional, and spiritual health.

5. Find meaning in adversity: Just as Mary found meaning in her experiences, we too can look for the lessons and growth opportunities in the challenges we face.

As we embrace our identity as resilient in Christ, we can face the challenges of life with confidence and courage. With hearts full of hope and trust in God's faithfulness, let us declare, "I am resilient."

Chapter 15 - I Am Resilient

Group/Individual Questions

What does resilience mean to you in your walk with God?

Can you share a time when you had to be resilient and how your faith played a role in that?

How has knowing that you are resilient in God changed your approach to setbacks?

What can you do to foster resilience?

How can you encourage resilience in others through your faith?

Chapter 16 - I am who God says I am

As we come to the conclusion of this journey of self-discovery, surrender and embracing our true identity in Christ, it is essential to remember that our foundation lies in the very nature of God Himself. When we understand who God is, we can trust what He says about us and confidently step into our purpose and calling.

In a moment of doubt and uncertainty, Moses found himself questioning his qualifications and capabilities to challenge Pharaoh and free the Hebrews. His concerns were indeed justified, given the magnitude of the task. However, in Exodus 3:14, God responded to Moses with a profound declaration: **"I AM WHO I AM."** This powerful statement not only reveals the eternal and unchanging nature of God but also affirms His sovereignty as the great **"I AM."** He is the source of all beings, the one who holds our lives and destinies in His hands, and the one who would empower Moses to fulfill his calling. Amazing, how this is the same God we have been talking about in the past chapters, and He is with you, right now.

Because we are created in His image and are His beloved children, we can trust that we are who God says we are. We can believe in His promises, hold fast to His truths, and walk in the fullness of our identity as women of God.

As we embrace our true identity in Christ and walk confidently in who God says we are, let us remember the words of renowned author, speaker and actress, Priscilla Shirer: "The enemy wants you to think that the absence of evidence is the evidence of absence. Don't believe his lies." Even when we can't see the tangible evidence of our worth and purpose, we can trust that God is at work and that our identity in Him is secure.

To live fully as who God says we are, let us remember these key principles:

1. Trust in God's unchanging nature: As the great "I AM," God is the same yesterday, today, and forever. We can rely on His faithfulness, love, and power to sustain us as we walk in our true identity.

2. Meditate on God's Word: Immerse yourself in Scripture, allowing the truth of God's promises and declarations about you to shape your thoughts, beliefs, and actions.

3. Pray for revelation and transformation: Ask the Holy Spirit to reveal any areas of your life where you need to embrace your identity in Christ more fully and to guide you in walking in the fullness of who God says you are.

4. Surround yourself with a godly community: Engage in fellowship with other believers who will support, encourage, and challenge you to grow in your understanding of your identity in Christ.

5. Share your story: Your testimony of embracing who God says you are can be an inspiration and encouragement to others. Look for opportunities to share your journey with those around you and when an opportunity arises, step out in obedience trusting that God will empower you to share your testimony.

As we step into our God-given identities, let us remember that our worth, purpose, and destiny are all found in the great "I AM." With confidence in His unchanging nature and love, we can boldly declare, "I am who God says I am."

Chapter 16 - I am who God says I am

Group/Individual Questions

What does it mean to you to embrace your identity in Christ?

Can you share a time when you felt a deep connection with your identity in Christ?

How has embracing your identity in Christ changed your life?

What can you do to live out your identity in Christ daily?

How can you help others embrace their true identity in Christ?

Concluding Words...

As we turn the last page of this book, I want you to know that I am incredibly proud of the journey you've embarked on. This journey of self-discovery, of embracing your identity in Christ, is not always an easy one, but it is profoundly rewarding.

Throughout these chapters, we've walked together through valleys of forgiveness, climbed mountains of courage, and rested in meadows of God's love. We've navigated the sometimes stormy seas of life, finding safety in God's protective love, healing in His touch, and freedom in His grace. We've celebrated being chosen, accepted, and loved by our Heavenly Father, and found contentment in His provision. We've faced our fears, recognized our beauty in His eyes, and harnessed His strength. We've stepped into our God-given authority, understood our value in His kingdom, and learned to bounce back with resilience.

But remember, this is not the end of your journey. It's a new beginning. A beginning of living out your true identity as God's beloved daughter, of walking in the freedom and purpose He has for you.

If you ever need a helping hand along the way, remember that there are resources available to you. At Therapeace Counseling, we offer an eBook on overcoming anxiety and a free anxiety guide , which can be invaluable tools on your journey. We also provide a free guide on Fair Fighting Rules for Communication in Relationships, which can help you navigate and improve your interpersonal relationships. And there will be many more books and resources on the way, especially tailored to men, written by my husband, Elias DaHora Jr.

For more personalized assistance, you can reach out to us at **TherapeaceCounseling.org** We are here to walk alongside you, to provide guidance and support as you continue to grow in your relationship with God and understanding of yourself.

If you're interested in diving deeper into the topics we've explored in this book or if you'd like to invite me for speaking engagements, please feel free to contact me at **Hello@therapeacecounseling.org**

Remember, you are who God says you are. You are His beloved daughter, chosen, loved, and wanted. Continue to walk in that truth, and let His love and grace guide you every step of the way.

With love and blessings,

Jackie Da Hora

Mental Health Tools and Spiritual Disciplines

Chapter 1: I Am Forgiven

- **Mental Health Tool:** Practice forgiveness exercises. For example, write down the situation you're having a hard time forgiving yourself for, then consciously decide to let it go and visualize it leaving your mind. Another tool is with your eyes and fists closed, imagine the situation where you're having a hard time receiving God's forgiveness: Take a deep breath through your nose (7 seconds) and let it out through your mouth slowly (7 seconds). "*God, please help me to receive your forgiveness …. I do not want to hold on to this anymore. I release all of this to you (open your fists), please give me your peace. I know you have forgiven me in Jesus' name, amen.*" You can do the same exercise and tailor it to asking God to help you forgive someone that has wronged you or a loved one.
- **Spiritual Discipline:** Meditate on scriptures that affirm God's forgiveness, such as 1 John 1:9.

Chapter 2: I Am Safe

- **Mental Health Tool:** Practice grounding techniques when feeling unsafe or anxious. For example, identify five things you can see, four things you can touch, three things you can hear, two things you can smell, and one thing you can taste. You can also listen to my 5 minute safe space guided imagery exercise on YouTube (search Therapeace Counseling) to help your mind create a safe space. This exercise focuses your imagination to create calm, peaceful images in your mind, thereby creating a "mental escape."

Peaceful imagery can stimulate changes in your heart rate, blood pressure, and respiratory patterns to help your body physically relax.

o **Spiritual Discipline:** Meditate on scriptures that affirm God's protection, such as Psalm 91.

Chapter 3: I Am Healed

o **Mental Health Tool:** Engage in art therapy or journaling to express and process emotions related to past hurts. For example, draw a picture that represents your hurt, then draw a picture that represents your healing.

o **Spiritual Discipline:** Practice the spiritual discipline of lament, pouring out your heart to God and waiting on His healing.

Chapter 4: I Am Called

o **Mental Health Tool:** Use career or personality assessments to gain insights into your strengths and passions. For example, take a free online assessment like the Myers-Briggs Type Indicator or a spiritual gifts assessment.

o **Spiritual Discipline:** Spend time in solitude and silence, listening for God's voice and direction. If this is difficult, try playing worship music, opening your bible and asking God to speak to you.

Chapter 5: I Am Free

- Mental Health Tool: Practice mindfulness to stay present and avoid being trapped by past regrets or future anxieties. For example, take a few minutes each day to focus on your breath and let go of distracting thoughts.

- Spiritual Discipline: Engage in fasting to break chains of dependence on anything other than God.

Chapter 6: I Am Loved

- Mental Health Tool: Use positive affirmations to reinforce your sense of self-worth and acceptance. For example, stand in front of a mirror each morning and say, "I am loved by God unconditionally."
- Spiritual Discipline: Practice the discipline of community, finding acceptance and belonging within the body of Christ.

Chapter 7: I Am Accepted

- Mental Health Tool: Practice saying an affirmation to yourself inspired by Ephesians 1:6. Add your name to the front. For example, "Jackie, you are accepted by Jesus."

- Spiritual Discipline: Meditate on scriptures that affirm your acceptance, such as Romans 15:7 and Colossians 1:21-22.

Chapter 8: I Am Chosen

- o **Mental Health Tool:** Practice self-compassion exercises to reinforce your inherent worth and chosenness. For example, write a compassionate letter to yourself acknowledging your worth and the fact that you are chosen by God.
- o **Spiritual Discipline:** Meditate on scriptures that affirm your chosenness, such as Jeremiah 1:5 and John 15:16.

Chapter 9: I Am Content

- o **Mental Health Tool:** Practice gratitude journaling to cultivate contentment. For example, each night before bed, write down three things you were grateful for that day.
- o **Spiritual Discipline:** Practice simplicity, finding contentment in God's provision rather than material possessions.

Chapter 10: I Am Courageous

- **Mental Health Tool:** Use visualization techniques to imagine successfully facing fears or challenges. For example, close your eyes and imagine a situation that scares you, then visualize yourself handling it with courage and success. Here is another tool: fear can paralyze us from being able to step into our God given purpose. Often, we will magnify our fears and the outcomes are irrational. Try this exercise to help you deconstruct your fear and reach a rational outcome:

- ○ Fear inducing thought / situation:
  _____

- ○ Worst case scenario:
  _____

- ○ Best case scenario:
  _____

- ○ Realistic outcome:
  _____

- **Spiritual Discipline:** Engage in prayer for courage, drawing on God's strength.

Chapter 11: I Am Beautiful

- **Mental Health Tool:** Practice body positivity exercises to embrace your physical appearance. For example, each day, find one thing you appreciate about your body and write it down or say out loud.
- **Spiritual Discipline:** Meditate on scriptures that affirm your beauty in God's eyes, such as Psalm 139:14.

Chapter 12: I Am Strong

- **Mental Health Tool:** Practice cognitive reframing techniques to shift your perspective and see challenges as opportunities for growth. For example, when faced with a difficult situation, instead of saying "I can't handle this," reframe it to "This is tough, but I can get through it with God's strength."
- **Spiritual Discipline:** Practice the discipline of perseverance, drawing on God's strength to endure challenges. Meditate on scriptures that affirm God's strength in you, such as Ephesians 6:10.

Chapter 13: I Am Empowered

- **Mental Health Tool:** Use assertiveness training techniques to express your needs and boundaries effectively. For example, practice using "I" statements to express your feelings and needs, such as "I feel... when you... and I need..."
- **Spiritual Discipline**: Engage in spiritual warfare prayers to exercise your authority in Christ and remember that boldness comes from abiding in Christ (Ephesians 6:10-18 and Ephesians 3:12).

Chapter 14: I Am Worthy

- **Mental Health Tool:** Practice self-love exercises to reinforce your sense of worth. For example, each day, do something kind for yourself, like taking a relaxing bath or reading a book you enjoy.
- **Spiritual Discipline:** Meditate on scriptures that affirm your worth, such as 1 Peter 2:9 and Matthew 10:29-31.

Chapter 15: I Am Resilient

- **Mental Health Tool:** Use resilience-building techniques. For example, practice reframing negative thoughts into positive ones, or engage in activities that help you relax and recharge.
- **Spiritual Discipline:** Practice the discipline of hope, trusting in God's strength to help you bounce back from adversity (Proverb 24:16).

Chapter 16: I Am Who God Says I Am

- **Mental Health Tool:** Use identity-affirming exercises. For example, create an "I am" list of positive attributes and strengths, such as "I am kind," "I am patient," or "I am a child of God."

- **Spiritual Discipline:** Meditate on scriptures that affirm your identity in Christ, such as 2 Corinthians 5:17, John 1:12, Ephesians 1:5, Romans 15:7, Colossians 2:9-10, 1 Corinthians 6:17. Romans 6:6, Genesis 1:27, Jeremiah 1:5, 1 Corinthians 12:27, 1 Peter 2:9, Galatians 3:27-28, 1 Corinthians 6:19-20, 1 John 3:1-2, Colossians 3:1-3

Steps to Reframing Negative Thoughts with Biblical Principles

1. Recognize the Negative Thought:

Before you can reframe a thought, you need to recognize it. When a negative thought enters your mind, pause and acknowledge it without judgment.

"Search me, O God, and know my heart! Try me and know my thoughts!" - Psalm 139:23 (ESV)

2. Challenge the Thought:

Ask yourself if the thought is true, if it's the worst-case scenario, and if there's another way to view the situation.

"We destroy arguments and every lofty opinion raised against the knowledge of God, and take every thought captive to obey Christ." - 2 Corinthians 10:5 (ESV)

3. Replace with Truth:

Find a scripture that challenges the negative thought. Memorize it, and when the negative thought arises, replace it with the scripture.

"Your word is a lamp to my feet and a light to my path." - Psalm 119:105 (ESV)

4. Practice Gratitude:

Shift your focus from what's going wrong to what's going right. Start a gratitude journal and list things you're thankful for daily.

"Give thanks in all circumstances; for this is the will of God in Christ Jesus for you." - 1 Thessalonians 5:18 (ESV)

5. Seek Community:

Share your struggles with trusted friends or a support group. They can offer encouragement, prayer, and a fresh perspective.

"Bear one another's burdens, and so fulfill the law of Christ." - Galatians 6:2 (ESV)

6. **Meditate and Pray:**

Spend time in prayer, asking God to renew your mind and give you His perspective. Meditate on scriptures that uplift and encourage you.

"Do not be anxious about anything, but in everything by prayer and supplication with thanksgiving let your requests be made known to God. And the peace of God, which surpasses all understanding, will guard your hearts and your minds in Christ Jesus." - Philippians 4:6-7 (ESV)

CONSIDER DONATING

Your support helps us provide free or discounted counseling and resources to those in need, and also supports our family, for which we are grateful.

Donate any amount securely via CashApp, Venmo, Zelle, or by mail at **www.TherapeaceCounseling.org/donate**

Or scan with your phone camera below…

Jackie DaHora, LCSW

Therapist, Speaker & Author

In our sessions together, I would help you identify what you'd like to change and create a plan to work towards it. It's a safe place where you can be yourself and not feel judged. As a Christian, I also offer prayer in our sessions and combine psychology with biblical principles. I look forward to working together. Take care.

Jackie DaHora

MODALITIES USED	COGNITIVE BEHAVIORAL THERAPY	SOLUTION FOCUSED BEHAVIORAL THERAPY	FAITH BASED CHRISTIAN THERAPY	MOTIVATIONAL INTERVIEWING
				TRAUMA-INFORMED CARE

I CAN HELP WITH...

- Anxiety
- Trauma
- Anger
- Self-harm
- Family dynamic issues
- Setting boundaries

- Communication skills
- Perfectionism
- People pleasing
- Finding a work-life balance
- Time management
- Changing unhelpful thoughts/beliefs
- Grounding exercises

SELF PAY ALSO ACCEPTED

Insurances accepted for FL, SC, TN Residents
Aetna, Oscar, Oxford Health Plans, UMR, UnitedHealthcare, UHC Student Resources, Blue Cross Blue Shield of Massachusetts, EAP Plans

THERAPEACE
COUNSELING

We can help you with :

Marital Counseling | Anxiety | Trauma | Anger | Depression | Stress | Relationship issues | Setting boundaries | Communication skills | Perfectionism | People pleasing | Finding a work-life balance | Relaxation techniques | Confidence building | College & Career Planning |

Health insurances accepted in FL, TN & SC :

✓ Aetna   ✓ Oxford Health Plans ✓ Oscar   ✓ UMR
✓ United Healthcare UHC | UBH ✓ UHC Student Resources ✓ UHC Global
✓ Employee Assistance Programs (Please visit our website for EAP list)

Out of pocket / Self pay accepted :

Please visit our website for cost and methods of payment.

Sessions are done via telehealth (video or phone)

Meet our Team

Jacquelin DaHora is a licensed psychotherapist. She provides therapy as well as life coaching to teens and adults. Faith based therapy offered per request. Also available for speaking opportunities.

Elias DaHora is a Board Certified Christian Counselor. He provides Christian counseling and life coaching. He also available for camps, conferences and workshops.

Visit our website to book a session

Hello@TheraPeaceCounseling.org | 305-925-0827
TheraPeaceCounseling.org

(What God Says) I Am:

Embracing My Identity as His Beloved Daughter

With questions at the end of each chapter for groups or personal study.

Written by: Jackie DaHora

TherapeaceCounseling.Org

Made in United States
Orlando, FL
10 February 2025

58337257R00059